T0063625

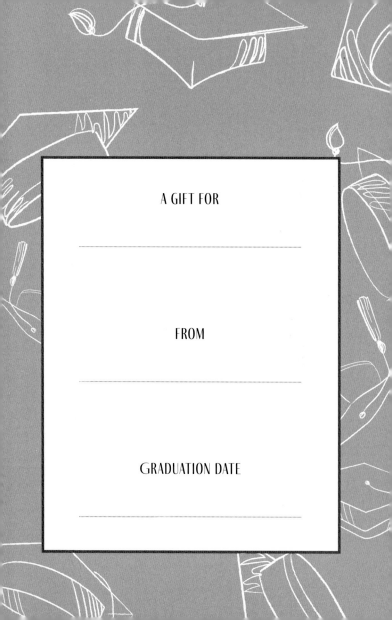

A GIFT FOR

....

FROM

....

GRADUATION DATE

....

— GOD'S GIFT FOR THE —

GRADUATE

— NKJV —

JACK COUNTRYMAN

COUNTRYMAN®

An Imprint of Thomas Nelson Publishers

THOMAS NELSON
Since 1798

God's Gift for the Graduate

© 2024 Jack Countryman

Published in Nashville, Tennessee, by Thomas Nelson. Thomas Nelson is a registered trademark of HarperCollins Christian Publishing, Inc.

Thomas Nelson titles may be purchased in bulk for educational, business, fund-raising, or sales promotional use. For information, please email SpecialMarkets@ThomasNelson.com.

Scripture quotations are from the New King James Version®. Copyright © 1982 by Thomas Nelson. Used by permission. All rights reserved.

Any internet addresses, phone numbers, or company or product information printed in this book are offered as a resource and are not intended in any way to be or to imply an endorsement by Thomas Nelson, nor does Thomas Nelson vouch for the existence, content, or services of these sites, phone numbers, companies, or products beyond the life of this book.

The information regarding the number of God's promises in the entry "God's Gift of His Promises" was found at Victor Knowles, "Promise and Fulfillment: Believing the Promises of God," *Leaven* 6, no. 3 (1998): article 4, https://digitalcommons.pepperdine.edu/leaven/vol6/iss3/4.

Cover design by Jonathan Maloney
Interior design by Kristy Edwards

ISBN: 978-1-4002-4317-4 (Audio)
ISBN: 978-1-4002-4316-7 (ePub)
ISBN: 978-1-4002-4309-9 (HC)

Printed in China

24 25 26 27 28 DSC 5 4 3 2 1

Contents

CONGRATULATIONS, GRADUATE!

Y ou are leaving school and headed into the next chapter of your life to make your mark. You'll face many challenges, and how you meet them will depend on the person you are and are becoming.

This book highlights the many gifts God has for you as you travel this character-forming path called life. He gives these gifts because He wants to bless you with His love, mercy, and grace each step of the way. He offers His guidance so you can live your best life in the center of His will.

As you read through this book, my prayer is that God will use it to ignite or reignite within you the desire to be all that He has called you to be. May you receive with gratitude the many gifts God has for you as you live each moment in His presence.

Jack Countryman

1

GOD'S GIFT OF LOVE

*L*ove. We carelessly throw around that word. We love pizza and puppies. And God.

God is love, and He commands us to love Him and to love our neighbors, even those who wrong us. He enables us to love with His love, a love that's sharply different from the world's. God's love refuses to run away; it weathers life's storms. His kind of love serves and sacrifices, blesses others and builds them up.

As God's transforming love makes us more like Jesus, our behaviors and attitudes should reflect His love. Toward that end, may His love take over your heart today.

I bow my knees to the Father of our Lord Jesus Christ . . . that He would grant you, according to the riches of His glory, to be strengthened with might through His Spirit in the inner man, that Christ may dwell in your hearts through faith; that you, being rooted and grounded in love, may be able to comprehend with all the saints what is the width and length and depth and height—to know the love of Christ which passes knowledge; that you may be filled with all the fullness of God.

EPHESIANS 3:14, 16–19

"God so loved the world that He gave His only begotten Son, that whoever believes in Him should not perish but have everlasting life. For God did not send His Son into the world to condemn the world, but that the world through Him might be saved."

JOHN 3:16–17

Let all that you do be done with love.

1 CORINTHIANS 16:14

Though I speak with the tongues of men and of angels, but have not love, I have become sounding brass or a clanging cymbal. And though I have the gift of prophecy, and understand all mysteries and all knowledge, and though I have all faith, so that I could remove mountains, but have not love, I am nothing. And though I bestow all my goods to feed the poor, and though I give my body to be burned, but have not love, it profits me nothing.

Love suffers long and is kind; love does not envy; love does not parade itself, is not puffed up; does not behave rudely, does not seek its own, is not provoked, thinks no evil; does not rejoice in iniquity, but rejoices in the truth; bears all things, believes all things, hopes all things, endures all things.

I CORINTHIANS 13:1–7

Let us love one another, for love is of God; and everyone who loves is born of God and knows God. He who does not love does not know God, for God is love. In this the love of God was manifested toward us, that God has sent His only begotten Son into the world, that we might live through Him. In this is love, not that we loved God, but that He loved us and sent His Son to be the propitiation for our sins. Beloved, if God so loved us, we also ought to love one another.

No one has seen God at any time. If we love one another, God abides in us, and His love has been perfected in us.

1 JOHN 4:7–12

Lord, in this new chapter, may I walk in Your amazing and indescribable love for me. Please fill me anew with Your Spirit so I can love others with Your gracious, persevering love. Amen.

2

GOD'S GIFT OF COMFORT

I n this fallen world, we will have troubles. Everyone experiences disappointment, loss, discouragement, and pain in life, and you won't be the exception. But know that God will comfort us always, including during stressful seasons of transition, and He does so because He loves us.

God also uses those tough times to give us wisdom about how to encourage the people around us who need His comfort. At those times, may we let Jesus guide our actions and our words as He uses us to be a comforter to others, a comforter who points them to Him, the perfect Comforter.

Blessed be the God and Father of our Lord Jesus Christ, the Father of mercies and God of all comfort, who comforts us in all our tribulation, that we may be able to comfort those who are in any trouble, with the comfort with which we ourselves are comforted by God. For as the sufferings of Christ abound in us, so our consolation also abounds through Christ.

2 CORINTHIANS 1:3–5

I thank my God, making mention of you always in my prayers, hearing of your love and faith which you have toward the Lord Jesus and toward all the saints, that the sharing of your faith may become effective by the acknowledgment of every good thing which is in you in Christ Jesus. For we have great joy and consolation in your love, because the hearts of the saints have been refreshed by you, brother.

PHILEMON 1:4–7

Now may our Lord Jesus Christ Himself, and our God and Father, who has loved us and given us everlasting consolation and good hope by grace, comfort your hearts and establish you in every good word and work.

2 THESSALONIANS 2:16–17

Do not think it strange concerning the fiery trial which is to try you, as though some strange thing happened to you; but rejoice to the extent that you partake of Christ's sufferings, that when His glory is revealed, you may also be glad with exceeding joy. If you are reproached for the name of Christ, blessed are you, for the Spirit of glory and of God rests upon you. . . . On your part He is glorified.

1 PETER 4:12–14

I will remember the works of the LORD;
Surely I will remember Your wonders
　　of old.
I will also meditate on all Your work,
And talk of Your deeds.
Your way, O God, is in the sanctuary;

Who is so great a God as our God?
You are the God who does wonders;
You have declared Your strength among
the peoples.
You have with Your arm redeemed Your
people,
The sons of Jacob and Joseph. *Selah*

PSALM 77:11–15

Lord, I thank You for being my faithful Comforter. I also thank You for blessing me with Your presence, giving me wisdom and compassion, and using me to comfort those around me. Amen.

3

GOD'S GIFT OF MERCY

*G*race is getting what we don't deserve. *Mercy* is *not* getting what we do deserve. And both are manifestations of God's great love for us.

God's loving-kindness, goodness, and mercy go hand in hand, revealing His character and inviting us to honor and glorify Him in every chapter of life. As we consider God's mercy, may His Holy Spirit reveal to us our sin so that we may confess it, receive the Lord's forgiveness, and go through the rest of the day rejoicing in His mercy and grace.

How wonderful is our God of mercy, of grace, and of everlasting love!

God shall send forth His mercy and His
    truth. . . .
Your mercy reaches unto the heavens,
And Your truth unto the clouds.

PSALM 57:3, 10

I will sing of Your power;
Yes, I will sing aloud of Your mercy in the
    morning;
For You have been my defense
And refuge in the day of my trouble.
To You, O my Strength, I will sing praises;
For God is my defense,
My God of mercy.

PSALM 59:16–17

Behold, the eye of the Lord is on those
    who fear Him,
On those who hope in His mercy. . . .
Our soul waits for the Lord;
He is our help and our shield. . . .
Let Your mercy, O Lord, be upon us,
Just as we hope in You.

PSALM 33:18, 20, 22

The LORD is my shepherd;
I shall not want. . . .
He leads me in the paths of righteousness
For His name's sake. . . .
Surely goodness and mercy shall follow
me
All the days of my life;
And I will dwell in the house of the LORD
Forever.

PSALM 23:1, 3, 6

Father, thank You for Your love, Your mercy, and Your grace. Please teach me to build my life on You and to live for You as I walk a new path and experience new situations. Amen.

4

GOD'S GIFT OF GRACE

A strikingly simple yet profound definition of *grace* is "undeserved favor." Think about that for a moment. What evidence of God's undeserved favor do you experience on any given day? What grace are you aware of even as you read this page?

Shelter, food, clothing. Family and friends. Our Savior and Scripture. The Holy Spirit and God's family. Mountains and oceans. Flowers and music.

Remember, all the joys we have in life—and all the beauty we find on this planet—are both because of and evidence of God's grace. Everything good in life is from Him. What amazing grace!

The Word became flesh and dwelt among us, and we beheld His glory, the glory as of the only begotten of the Father, full of grace and truth. . . . And of His fullness we have all received, and grace for grace. For the law was given through Moses, but grace and truth came through Jesus Christ. No one has seen God at any time. The only begotten Son, who is in the bosom of the Father, He has declared Him.

JOHN 1:14, 16–18

Moses said to the LORD . . . "You have said, 'I know you by name, and you have also found grace in My sight.' Now therefore, I pray, if I have found grace in Your sight, show me now Your way, that I may know You and that I may find grace in Your sight."

EXODUS 33:12–13

"I will be gracious to whom I will be gracious, and I will have compassion on whom I will have compassion."

EXODUS 33:19

The LORD God is a sun and shield;
The LORD will give grace and glory;
No good thing will He withhold
From those who walk uprightly.
O LORD of hosts,
Blessed is the man who trusts in You!

PSALM 84:11–12

All have sinned and fall short of the glory of God, being justified freely by His grace through the redemption that is in Christ Jesus, whom God set forth as a propitiation by His blood, through faith, to demonstrate His righteousness.

ROMANS 3:23–25

God of grace, Your gifts to me are beyond counting and beyond description. Thank You for pouring Your undeserved favor into my life. May Your extravagant grace to me forever be a source of joy! Amen.

5

GOD'S GIFT OF HOPE IN HIM

In a world of darkness and pain, of mindless routines and constant demands, life can seem pointless. Yet our God of hope gives us reasons to get out of bed in the morning. As His Word declares, He is our hiding place, our shield, our refuge, and our hope. Nothing you'll face is impossible for Him, and no past experience is beyond His redemption. Find hope in His life-giving Word, in remembering His great faithfulness, and in His everyday provision for your body, soul, and spirit. Our resurrected Lord gives us hope for today, for new chapters, and for eternity.

I wait for the LORD, my soul waits,

And in His word I do hope.

My soul waits for the Lord

More than those who watch for the
morning—

Yes, more than those who watch for the
morning.

O Israel, hope in the LORD;

For with the LORD there is mercy,

And with Him is abundant redemption.

PSALM 130:5–7

Behold, the eye of the LORD is on those
who fear Him,

On those who hope in His mercy. . . .

Our soul waits for the LORD;

He is our help and our shield.

For our heart shall rejoice in Him,

Because we have trusted in His
holy name.

PSALM 33:18, 20–21

You are my hope, O Lord God;
You are my trust from my youth.
By You I have been upheld from birth;
You are He who took me out of my
      mother's womb.
My praise shall be continually of You.

PSALM 71:5–6

"Blessed is the man who trusts in the
      Lord,
And whose hope is the Lord.
For he shall be like a tree planted by the
      waters,
Which spreads out its roots by the river,
And will not fear when heat comes;
But its leaf will be green,
And will not be anxious in the year of
      drought,
Nor will cease from yielding fruit."

JEREMIAH 17:7–8

Be of good courage,
And He shall strengthen your heart,
All you who hope in the LORD.

PSALM 31:24

*Almighty God, in You alone I find
hope for today, hope for tomorrow,
and hope for eternity! You are the
same yesterday, today, and forever.
That's why I find great and unshakable
hope in Your faithfulness. Amen.*

6

God's Gift of Forgiveness

The Lord's gift of forgiveness covers all our sins: those words and deeds we're so comfortable with that we don't recognize them as sin; those times we know we're sinning, choosing our way instead of God's; and everything in between. We should be profoundly grateful for God's forgiveness, yet we easily take it for granted—until we struggle to forgive people who hurt us. In this next chapter of your life, you may find yourself needing to forgive bigger hurts than ever before. Rely on God to give you the grace to forgive in the same way He has forgiven you.

As far as the east is from the west,
So far has He removed our transgressions
from us.

PSALM 103:12

Blessed is the man to whom the LORD
does not impute iniquity,
And in whose spirit there is no deceit.
When I kept silent, my bones grew old
Through my groaning all the day long.
For day and night Your hand was heavy
upon me;
My vitality was turned into the drought of
summer. *Selah*
I acknowledged my sin to You,
And my iniquity I have not hidden.
I said, "I will confess my transgressions to
the LORD,"
And You forgave the iniquity of my sin.
Selah

PSALM 32:2–5

If we say that we have no sin, we deceive our-selves, and the truth is not in us. If we confess our sins, He is faithful and just to forgive us our sins and to cleanse us from all unrighteousness.

1 JOHN 1:8–9

Bless the Lord, O my soul,
And forget not all His benefits:
Who forgives all your iniquities,
Who heals all your diseases,
Who redeems your life from destruction,
Who crowns you with lovingkindness and
    tender mercies.

PSALM 103:2–4

In Him we have redemption through His blood, the forgiveness of sins, according to the riches of His grace.

EPHESIANS 1:7

Father, when I reflect on Your forgiveness of my sins—words, thoughts, and deeds—I am humbled by Your mercy and grace. Please help me extend such grace to those people I need to forgive. Amen.

7

GOD'S GIFT OF PATIENCE

God, our perfect Parent, is patient with us, His imperfect children. He is slow to anger when we are slow to repent, and He "suffers long" when we need to keep learning the same lessons of trust and obedience. In this next—and probably fuller, busier, and more stressful—chapter of your life, God will be patient when your regular time with Him slips, when you doubt His faithfulness, and when you choose to go your own way instead of staying on His narrow path for you. God will always be patient, slow to anger, and abounding in kindness and love.

I know that You are a gracious and merciful
God, slow to anger and abundant in lovingkindness, One who relents from doing harm.

JONAH 4:2

You are God,
Ready to pardon,
Gracious and merciful,
Slow to anger,
Abundant in kindness.

NEHEMIAH 9:17

The LORD is merciful and gracious,
Slow to anger, and abounding in mercy.

PSALM 103:8

The LORD is gracious and full of
    compassion,
Slow to anger and great in mercy.
The LORD is good to all,
And His tender mercies are over all His
    works.

PSALM 145:8–9

Love suffers long and is kind.

1 CORINTHIANS 13:4

Lord, thank You for Your patience with me. Please enable me to extend to others the kind of patience You show me. Help me to be slow to anger and quick to forgive. Amen.

8

GOD'S GIFT OF DIRECTION

Like every good parent, our heavenly Father has given us instructions for our own good. He wants to direct our steps and inform our thoughts and words. In addition to the Bible that sets forth His desires for us, He gives His Holy Spirit to enable us to remember His directions, to act accordingly, and to walk the narrow path that gives life and that honors Him. May all that you say and do impact people around you— people you've known for a long time and people you'll meet in this new chapter—with the light and love of our Lord.

"What does the LORD your God require of you, but to fear the LORD your God, to walk in all His ways and to love Him, to serve the LORD your God with all your heart and with all your soul, and to keep the commandments of the LORD and His statutes which I command you today for your good?"

DEUTERONOMY 10:12–13

Be doers of the word, and not hearers only.

JAMES 1:22

Rejoice always, pray without ceasing, in everything give thanks; for this is the will of God in Christ Jesus for you.

1 THESSALONIANS 5:16–18

Take careful heed to do the commandment and the law which Moses the servant of the LORD commanded you, to love the LORD your God, to walk in all His ways, to keep His commandments, to hold fast to Him, and to serve Him with all your heart and with all your soul.

JOSHUA 22:5

Whatever you do, do it heartily, as to the Lord and not to men.

COLOSSIANS 3:23

Father, I want Your directions to guide the words I speak, the decisions I make, and the way I treat people. May all I say and do shine Your light and reflect Your love. Amen.

9

GOD'S GIFT OF FAITH

God's gift of faith secures our greatest graduation of all: our graduation into heaven for eternity. This faith that saves us from eternal separation from God—that's the essence of hell—is the recognition that Jesus took the punishment for our sins, died in our place, and then rose from the dead, victorious over sin and death. We receive God's gift of faith when we accept this truth about Jesus and welcome Him as our personal Savior. Walking through a life with Jesus is a beautiful gift of God's grace and love for now—as you leave school—and forever.

Having been justified by faith, we have peace with God through our Lord Jesus Christ, through whom also we have access by faith into this grace in which we stand, and rejoice in hope of the glory of God.

ROMANS 5:1–2

I am not ashamed of the gospel of Christ, for it is the power of God to salvation for everyone who believes. . . . For in it the righteousness of God is revealed from faith to faith; as it is written, "The just shall live by faith."

ROMANS 1:16–17

Count it all joy when you fall into various trials, knowing that the testing of your faith produces patience. But let patience have its perfect work, that you may be perfect and complete, lacking nothing.

JAMES 1:2–4

I have been crucified with Christ; it is no longer I who live, but Christ lives in me; and the life which I now live in the flesh I live by faith in the Son of God, who loved me and gave Himself for me.

GALATIANS 2:20

"Do not worry about your life, what you will eat; nor about the body, what you will put on. Life is more than food, and the body is more than clothing. Consider the ravens, for they neither sow nor reap, which have neither storehouse nor barn; and God feeds them. Of how much more value are you than the birds? And which of you by worrying can add one cubit to his stature? If you then are not able to do the least, why are you anxious for the rest? Consider the lilies, how they grow: they neither toil nor spin; and yet I say to you, even Solomon in all his glory was not arrayed like one of these. If then God so clothes the grass, which today is in the field and tomorrow is thrown into the oven, how much more will He clothe you, O you of little faith?"

LUKE 12:22–28

Lord, no words are sufficient to thank You for the gift of faith. May I live in a way that honors You and reflects my gratitude for the eternal gift of saving faith. Amen.

10

GOD'S GIFT OF HIS POWER

Throughout its pages, the Word of God declares His power over creation and history, over governments and demons. May our lives reflect our respect for Him who is infinite in power, Him whom we rightly praise as almighty, omnipotent, and sovereign. This all-powerful God, however, doesn't keep His power to Himself. He graciously gives His people the power we need to answer His call on our lives, to glorify Him in all we do, and to love with His love. May you rely on His power in every moment of every day in this new chapter of your life!

Who is God, except the Lord?
And who is a rock, except our God?
God is my strength and power,
And He makes my way perfect.
He makes my feet like the feet of deer,
And sets me on my high places.

2 SAMUEL 22:32–34

[The Lord] said to me [Paul], "My grace is sufficient for you, for My strength is made perfect in weakness." Therefore most gladly I will rather boast in my infirmities, that the power of Christ may rest upon me.

2 CORINTHIANS 12:9

Blessed are You, Lord God of Israel, our
Father, forever and ever. . . .
In Your hand is power and might;
In Your hand it is to make great
And to give strength to all.

1 CHRONICLES 29:10, 12

Ascribe strength to God;
His excellence is over Israel,
And His strength is in the clouds.
O God, You are more awesome than Your
    holy places.
The God of Israel is He who gives
    strength and power to His people.

PSALM 68:34–35

Ah, Lord GOD! Behold, You have made the heavens and the earth by Your great power and outstretched arm. There is nothing too hard for You.

JEREMIAH 32:17

Father, when I think of Your power and sovereign control over every aspect of life, I am overcome with awe. May I never lose that awe and always come humbly before Your throne of grace. Amen.

11

God's Gift of His Goodness

The Lord's immeasurable goodness is reflected in the variety of ways He shows us His love. Each and every day He blesses us with a place to live, food to eat, and a job to do. He gives us purpose in life, His truth as a foundation for life, peace in our hearts, and the invitation into a life-giving relationship with Him. He forgives our sin and redeems our missteps. He sends us out, guides us, and walks with us—as you will experience throughout this new chapter of your life. What a wonderful Savior is Jesus our Lord!

Oh, taste and see that the LORD is good;
Blessed is the man who trusts in Him!

PSALM 34:8

The word of the LORD is right,
And all His work is done in truth.
He loves righteousness and justice;
The earth is full of the goodness of
      the LORD.

PSALM 33:4–5

The goodness of God leads you to repentance.

ROMANS 2:4

Oh, give thanks to the LORD, for He is
      good!
For His mercy endures forever. . . .
Oh, that men would give thanks to the
      LORD for His goodness,
And for His wonderful works to the
      children of men!
For He satisfies the longing soul,
And fills the hungry soul with goodness.

PSALM 107:1, 8–9

You, Lord, are good, and ready to forgive,
And abundant in mercy to all those who
call upon You.

PSALM 86:5

*Lord, You are infinitely good. You
bless me daily with Your love, mercy,
grace, provision, guidance, peace,
hope, presence—and that list is
incomplete. You are good, and You
are good to me. Thank You! Amen.*

12

God's Gift of His Truth

Graduate, as you have undoubtedly heard and will continue to hear, people today talk about "my truth." Let me suggest that as you establish a life for yourself, you search the Scriptures for truth—for proven, unchanging, rock-solid truth. God wants you to know Jesus—who *is* Truth—so that you can experience life as He designed it, life in relationship with Him. When you find Jesus and truth, you will also find freedom from the deception and pitfalls of the world. You will find joy, hope, and peace, and you will know abundant life, whatever circumstances you encounter.

Jesus said to [Thomas], "I am the way, the truth, and the life. No one comes to the Father except through Me."

JOHN 14:6

Jesus said to those Jews who believed Him, "If you abide in My word, you are My disciples indeed. And you shall know the truth, and the truth shall make you free."

JOHN 8:31–32

If we say that we have fellowship with [God], and walk in darkness, we lie and do not practice the truth. But if we walk in the light as He is in the light, we have fellowship with one another, and the blood of Jesus Christ His Son cleanses us from all sin.

If we say that we have no sin, we deceive ourselves, and the truth is not in us. If we confess our sins, He is faithful and just to forgive us our sins and to cleanse us from all unrighteousness.

1 JOHN 1:6–9

Show me Your ways, O Lord;
Teach me Your paths.
Lead me in Your truth and teach me,
For You are the God of my salvation.

PSALM 25:4–5

Teach me Your way, O Lord;
I will walk in Your truth.

PSALM 86:11

*Holy Spirit, I ask You to help me recognize
the Enemy's lies, embrace divine and
eternal truth, and walk in the freedom
it offers. In every chapter of life, guide
me according to Your truth. Amen.*

13

GOD'S GIFT OF CONFIDENCE IN HIM

Confidence in the rightness of our choice to name Jesus as Lord and to trust Him with our life truly is a gift from God. We can, with complete confidence, place every season of life in His hands and depend on Him for all we need. Jesus will definitely provide truth and guidance as well as food and clothes. We can be absolutely confident, too, of spending eternity with Him. Among the fruit of this confidence is His peace that passes understanding. Start every day by declaring with confidence your trust in your faithful God. He will not let you down.

I called on the LORD in distress;
The LORD answered me and set me in a
    broad place.
The LORD is on my side;
I will not fear.
What can man do to me? . . .
It is better to trust in the LORD
Than to put confidence in man.
It is better to trust in the LORD
Than to put confidence in princes.

PSALM 118:5–6, 8–9

Thus says the Lord GOD, the Holy One of
    Israel:
"In returning and rest you shall be saved;
In quietness and confidence shall be your
    strength."

ISAIAH 30:15

Abide in [Jesus], that when He appears, we may
have confidence and not be ashamed before
Him at His coming.

1 JOHN 2:28

Keep sound wisdom and discretion;
So they will be life to your soul
And grace to your neck.
Then you will walk safely in your way,
And your foot will not stumble. . . .
The LORD will be your confidence,
And will keep your foot from being
   caught.

PROVERBS 3:21–23, 26

To me . . . this grace was given, that I should preach among the Gentiles the unsearchable riches of Christ . . . that now the manifold wisdom of God might be made known by the church . . . according to the eternal purpose which He accomplished in Christ Jesus our Lord, in whom we have boldness and access with confidence through faith in Him.

EPHESIANS 3:8, 10–12

Lord, great is Your faithfulness. Rock-solid are Your promises. Ever-present is Your Spirit. I can with confidence walk through life with You, trusting You to guide me, provide for me, and always love me. Amen.

14

GOD'S GIFT OF HIS PROTECTION

This world offers plenty of forces, circumstances, and ideas that we need protection from. Those of us who have placed our lives in God's hands are blessed by His promises to protect us. We also find in His Word the encouraging testimonies of people He has protected. Consider the amazing descriptions of God in today's verses. *Rock, fortress, shield, stronghold, refuge,* and *tower* imply battle, but softer images also reflect God's protection: angel hands lift us up, and we find shelter under God's wings. Whatever unknowns lie ahead, you can rely on God's protection.

The Lord is my rock and my fortress and
        my deliverer;
My God, my strength, in whom I will trust;
My shield and the horn of my salvation,
        my stronghold.
I will call upon the Lord, who is worthy to
        be praised;
So shall I be saved from my enemies.

PSALM 18:2–3

My soul trusts in You;
And in the shadow of Your wings I will
        make my refuge.

PSALM 57:1

He shall cover you with His feathers,
And under His wings you shall take
        refuge;
His truth shall be your shield and buckler.
You shall not be afraid of the terror by
        night,
Nor of the arrow that flies by day.

PSALM 91:4–5

Because you have made the LORD, who is
    my refuge,
Even the Most High, your dwelling place,
No evil shall befall you,
Nor shall any plague come near your
    dwelling;
For He shall give His angels charge
    over you,
To keep you in all your ways.
In their hands they shall bear you up.

PSALM 91:9–12

You have been a shelter for me,
A strong tower from the enemy.
I will abide in Your tabernacle forever;
I will trust in the shelter of Your wings.

PSALM 61:3–4

Lord, I thank You, my Fortress and Refuge, for protecting me from threats I'm aware of and those I'm not. I praise You for being with me whatever I encounter in life. Amen.

15

GOD'S GIFT OF SURRENDER

We probably can't appreciate the significance of the title *Lord*. The lord of a realm required his people to yield their will and surrender themselves to his wishes. Naming Jesus as Lord therefore means relinquishing our pride, yielding our will, and surrendering ourselves to His plans, desires, and values. That assignment may be tough at times, but God will not take second place in our lives. Why would we even want our own ideas to take precedence over those of our all-wise, all-loving God? Know that coming under Jesus' lordship will bring the gifts of guidance, peace, and freedom.

Submit to God. Resist the devil and he will flee from you. Draw near to God and He will draw near to you.

JAMES 4:7–8

"Our Father in heaven,
Hallowed be Your name.
Your kingdom come.
Your will be done
On earth as it is in heaven."

MATTHEW 6:9–10

Let nothing be done through selfish ambition or conceit, but in lowliness of mind let each esteem others better than himself. Let each of you look out not only for his own interests, but also for the interests of others.

PHILIPPIANS 2:3–4

Therefore humble yourselves under the mighty hand of God, that He may exalt you in due time.

1 PETER 5:5–6

All of you be submissive to one another, and be clothed with humility, for

> "God resists the proud,
> But gives grace to the humble."

Let every soul be subject to the governing authorities. For there is no authority except from God, and the authorities that exist are appointed by God.

ROMANS 13:1

Lord, You know my heart better than I do. You know those areas of my heart and my life that I'm not surrendering to You. Please help me trust and let go. Amen.

16

GOD'S GIFT OF
ANSWERED PRAYER

Our good and gracious God gives us many reasons to praise and thank Him. Seeing Him answer our prayers is one such reason. Granted, our heavenly Father's answer may be *no* or *not yet* rather than an immediate and resounding *yes*. The fact remains, though, that we have the amazing privilege of approaching His throne and asking Him for whatever is on our hearts. In addition to hearing us, He blesses us by answering those prayers. May we pray with expectation in every season of life—and may we always be quick to thank Him when we recognize His answers.

"Ask, and it will be given to you; seek, and you will find; knock, and it will be opened to you. For everyone who asks receives, and he who seeks finds, and to him who knocks it will be opened. Or what man is there among you who, if his son asks for bread, will give him a stone? Or if he asks for a fish, will he give him a serpent? If you then, being evil, know how to give good gifts to your children, how much more will your Father who is in heaven give good things to those who ask Him!"

MATTHEW 7:7–11

The LORD is my strength and my shield;
My heart trusted in Him, and I am helped;
Therefore my heart greatly rejoices,
And with my song I will praise Him.

PSALM 28:7

"Whatever you ask in My name, that I will do, that the Father may be glorified in the Son. If you ask anything in My name, I will do it."

JOHN 14:13–14

O Lord my God, I cried out to You,
And You healed me.
O Lord, You brought my soul up from the
    grave;
You have kept me alive, that I should not
    go down to the pit.

PSALM 30:2–3

Solomon stood before the altar of the Lord in the presence of all the assembly of Israel, and spread out his hands toward heaven; and he said: "Lord God of Israel, there is no God in heaven above or on earth below like You, who keep Your covenant and mercy with Your servants who walk before You with all their hearts. You have kept what You promised Your servant David my father; You have both spoken with Your mouth and fulfilled it with Your hand."

1 KINGS 8:22–24

Father, thank You for the privilege of
prayer. Please teach me to pray with greater
faith, to recognize Your voice, to watch for
Your answers with greater expectation,
and to thank You with greater joy. Amen.

17

GOD'S GIFT OF HIS
WILL FOR YOUR LIFE

As you leave school and enter a new season of
life, may you continue to pray, "Thy will be
done." Knowing God's will requires nurturing
your relationship with Him and walking closely
with Him. Having named Jesus as your Lord,
remember who—and remember whose—you
are. Life will throw many temptations, challenges, and sources of stress your way, and the
strength of your relationship with God will
affect your faithfulness to His will for your life,
which He doesn't hide but sets forth in Scripture.
May you choose the blessings of living according to God's will and His ways.

Rejoice always, pray without ceasing, in everything give thanks; for this is the will of God in Christ Jesus for you.

1 THESSALONIANS 5:16–18

Do not be conformed to this world, but be transformed by the renewing of your mind, that you may prove what is that good and acceptable and perfect will of God.

ROMANS 12:2

[Jesus] looked around in a circle at those who sat about Him, and said, "Here are My mother and My brothers! For whoever does the will of God is My brother and My sister and mother."

MARK 3:34–35

Trust in the Lord with all your heart,
And lean not on your own understanding;
In all your ways acknowledge Him,
And He shall direct your paths.

PROVERBS 3:5–6

Lord, help me to always lean on You and Your Word in my effort to live according to Your will. I want to be faithful to You every day and in every chapter of my life. Amen.

18

GOD'S GIFT OF THE HOLY SPIRIT

Y ou are starting a new adventure! Remember that when God calls you to a new role or task, He will empower you to do what you need to do. By the power of His Holy Spirit, who is within you if you've named Jesus your Lord, you will have guidance, strength, wisdom, and even joy. The Spirit helps you recall God's truth when you need it, and perhaps most wonderful of all, He prays for you when you don't know how to pray. So embrace the adventure knowing that Jesus' Spirit within you will help each step of the way.

The Spirit also helps in our weaknesses. For we do not know what we should pray for as we ought, but the Spirit Himself makes intercession for us with groanings which cannot be uttered. Now He who searches the hearts knows what the mind of the Spirit is, because He makes intercession for the saints according to the will of God.

ROMANS 8:26–27

"The Helper, the Holy Spirit, whom the Father will send in My name, He will teach you all things, and bring to your remembrance all things that I said to you."

JOHN 14:26

"When He, the Spirit of truth, has come, He will guide you into all truth; for He will not speak on His own authority, but whatever He hears He will speak; and He will tell you things to come. He will glorify Me, for He will take of what is Mine and declare it to you."

JOHN 16:13–14

As many as are led by the Spirit of God, these are sons of God. For you did not receive the spirit of bondage again to fear, but you received the Spirit of adoption by whom we cry out, "Abba, Father." The Spirit Himself bears witness with our spirit that we are children of God.

ROMANS 8:14–16

"You shall be baptized with the Holy Spirit not many days from now.... You shall receive power when the Holy Spirit has come upon you; and you shall be witnesses to Me in Jerusalem, and in all Judea and Samaria, and to the end of the earth."

ACTS 1:5, 8

Lord, thank You for the gift of Your Holy Spirit. May I be sensitive to His guidance and rely on His strength so I honor You in everything I say and do. Amen.

19

GOD'S GIFT OF FREEDOM

When we accept Jesus Christ as our personal Savior, we receive the gift of freedom from the eternal consequences of our sin, the eternal consequences of going our own way instead of walking in the way the Lord has established for His people. We find freedom from purpose-lessness, cynicism, and bondage to sin and the desires of the flesh. We also find freedom in serving the Lord and the freedom to love the people He places in our lives to love. Forgiven of our sin, we can experience the freedom and the joy of living in the light.

Jesus said to those Jews who believed Him, "If you abide in My word, you are My disciples indeed. And you shall know the truth, and the truth shall make you free."

JOHN 8:31–32

As through one man's offense judgment came to all men, resulting in condemnation, even so through one Man's righteous act the free gift came to all men, resulting in justification of life.

ROMANS 5:18

"If the Son makes you free, you shall be free indeed."

JOHN 8:36

You, brethren, have been called to liberty; only do not use liberty as an opportunity for the flesh, but through love serve one another. For all the law is fulfilled in one word, even in this: "You shall love your neighbor as yourself."

GALATIANS 5:13–14

Having been set free from sin, you became slaves of righteousness. . . . Just as you presented your members as slaves of uncleanness, and of lawlessness leading to more lawlessness, so now present your members as slaves of righteousness for holiness. . . . Now having been set free from sin, and having become slaves of God, you have your fruit to holiness, and the end, everlasting life.

ROMANS 6:18–19, 22

Thank You, Lord, for the freedom of forgiveness, of knowing Your truth, and of choosing Your boundaries. Thank You for the freedom to love and serve You. May I use my freedom to bring You glory. Amen.

20

GOD'S GIFT OF SPIRITUAL HEALING

In the following verses, pay attention to how God's healing isn't limited to physical needs. You've undoubtedly noticed that life is difficult, that all of us wound and are wounded. When we don't experience healing, we will continue to wound others and even ourselves. Whatever wounds you carry now and whatever you sustain in the future, know that God brings healing to any and every wound. Sometimes He provides healing through the wisdom and care of medical professionals; sometimes He heals the wound with His mighty power without an intermediary. May you always pray boldly for healing of all kinds!

[Jesus] healed those who had need of healing.

LUKE 9:11

[Jesus] Himself bore our sins in His own body on the tree, that we, having died to sins, might live for righteousness—by whose stripes you were healed.

1 PETER 2:24

Jesus went about all Galilee, teaching in their synagogues, preaching the gospel of the kingdom, and healing all kinds of sickness and all kinds of disease among the people. Then His fame went throughout all Syria; and they brought to Him all sick people who were afflicted with various diseases and torments, and those who were demon-possessed, epileptics, and paralytics; and He healed them.

MATTHEW 4:23–24

He heals the brokenhearted
And binds up their wounds.

PSALM 147:3

God anointed Jesus of Nazareth with the Holy Spirit and with power, who went about doing good and healing all who were oppressed by the devil, for God was with Him.

ACTS 10:38

Heavenly Father and Great Physician, I praise You that Your healing power is unlimited: You can heal all my wounds, whether they are physical, emotional, psychological, relational, or spiritual. I praise and thank You! Amen.

21

GOD'S GIFT OF
OUR INHERITANCE

So what is the inheritance that God has for His children? Simply put, our inheritance is heaven. Made available to us by the sacrificial death of Jesus in payment for our sins, heaven is a place free of tears and pain. It is an existence of joy and fulfillment in God's glorious presence. Heaven is the eternal dwelling place for our God as well as for us. In that sense, we are His inheritance just as His heavenly home is our inheritance. Once we name Jesus as our Lord, nothing can take away that promised inheritance of life eternal with Him!

O LORD, You are the portion of my
     inheritance and my cup;
You maintain my lot.
The lines have fallen to me in pleasant
     places;
Yes, I have a good inheritance. . . .
In Your presence is fullness of joy;
At Your right hand are pleasures
     forevermore.

PSALM 16:5–6, 11

The LORD knows the days of the upright,
And their inheritance shall be forever.

PSALM 37:18

[Jesus] is the Mediator of the new covenant, by means of death, for the redemption of the transgressions under the first covenant, that those who are called may receive the promise of the eternal inheritance.

HEBREWS 9:15

In [Jesus] you also trusted, after you heard the word of truth, the gospel of your salvation; in whom also, having believed, you were sealed with the Holy Spirit of promise, who is the guarantee of our inheritance until the redemption of the purchased possession, to the praise of His glory.

EPHESIANS 1:13–14

Behold, the tabernacle of God is with men, and He will dwell with them, and they shall be His people. God Himself will be with them and be their God. And God will wipe away every tear from their eyes; there shall be no more death, nor sorrow, nor crying. There shall be no more pain, for the former things have passed away.

REVELATION 21:3–4

Lord Jesus, thank You for the promised inheritance of eternal life with You in heaven. Aware of its great cost, I am humbled by the fact that You want me to spend eternity with You. Amen.

22

GOD'S GIFT OF HIS PROMISES

Did you know that God has made more than seven thousand promises to His people? Through the millennia, God's promises have reflected His love for us, His good plans for us, the blessings He longs to bestow, and His encouragement to live according to His guidelines. In Scripture we have seen God make and keep promises: His sending us a Savior is the greatest fulfilled promise ever (Genesis 3:15). His Son promised to send the Holy Spirit, and He kept that promise (Acts 2:1–4). And the list continues! God is both Promise Maker and Promise Keeper—and we are the beneficiaries!

As God has said:

> "I will dwell in them
> And walk among them.
> I will be their God,
> And they shall be My people."

Therefore

> "Come out from among them
> And be separate, says the Lord.
> Do not touch what is unclean,
> And I will receive you."
> "I will be a Father to you,
> And you shall be My sons and daughters,

> Says the Lord Almighty."
>
> 2 CORINTHIANS 6:16–18

Let us hold fast the confession of our hope without wavering, for He who promised is faithful.

HEBREWS 10:23

The LORD God said to the serpent . . .
"I will put enmity
Between you and the woman,
And between your seed and her Seed;
He shall bruise your head,
And you shall bruise His heel."

GENESIS 3:14–15

As God is faithful, our word to you was not Yes and No. For the Son of God, Jesus Christ, who was preached among you by us—by me, Silvanus, and Timothy—was not Yes and No, but in Him was Yes. For all the promises of God in Him are Yes, and in Him Amen, to the glory of God through us. Now He who establishes us with you in Christ and has anointed us is God, who also has sealed us and given us the Spirit in our hearts as a guarantee.

2 CORINTHIANS 1:18–22

"If you love Me, keep My commandments. And I will pray the Father, and He will give you another Helper, that He may abide with you forever—the Spirit of truth, whom the world cannot receive, because it neither sees Him nor knows Him; but you know Him, for He dwells with you and will be in you. I will not leave you orphans; I will come to you."

JOHN 14:15–18

Almighty God, You promised a Savior, the Holy Spirit, and Your presence with me always. You have kept these and many other promises. I know Your great faithfulness will continue wherever life takes me. Amen.

23

GOD'S GIFT OF PEACE

First, the most significant peace any of us can know is the eternal peace that comes with our justification: we have peace with our holy God because of Jesus' death on the cross on our behalf. But as today's verses reflect, our gracious God has peace for us in the day to day as well as for eternity. Whatever conflict and upheaval we see in the world at large and whatever pressure and stress we ourselves are experiencing, we can know the peace of God. His peace helps us recognize His presence with us, and we can know comfort and hope.

The LORD will give strength to His people;
The LORD will bless His people with peace.
PSALM 29:11

Be anxious for nothing, but in everything by prayer and supplication, with thanksgiving, let your requests be made known to God; and the peace of God, which surpasses all understanding, will guard your hearts and minds through Christ Jesus.
PHILIPPIANS 4:6–7

You will keep him in perfect peace,
Whose mind is stayed on You.
ISAIAH 26:3

May the God of hope fill you with all joy and peace in believing, that you may abound in hope by the power of the Holy Spirit.
ROMANS 15:13

"Peace I leave with you, My peace I give to you; not as the world gives do I give to you. Let not your heart be troubled, neither let it be afraid."

JOHN 14:27

Father, Your gift of peace is so timely in this season of transition and question marks and new experiences. Please teach me the life lesson of knowing Your peace despite the circumstances of my life. Amen.

24

GOD'S GIFT OF STRENGTH

God's greatest command is "Love the LORD your God with all your heart, with all your soul, and with all your strength" (Deuteronomy 6:5). By design, our gracious God gives us His strength, so we are able to obey this and every command He issues. All His commands are for our good, and we need His strength if we are to obey each one. God's strength also enables us to stand strong against our Enemy and against the evil in the world. Wait on the Lord for His strength and find yourself mounting up on wings like eagles!

The LORD is my strength and my shield;
My heart trusted in Him, and I am
    helped. . . .
The LORD is their strength,
And He is the saving refuge of His
    anointed.

PSALM 28:7–8

The LORD will give strength to His people;
The LORD will bless His people with peace.

PSALM 29:11

He gives power to the weak,
And to those who have no might He
    increases strength. . . .
Those who wait on the LORD
Shall renew their strength;
They shall mount up with wings like
    eagles,
They shall run and not be weary,
They shall walk and not faint.

ISAIAH 40:29, 31

The LORD is my rock and my fortress and
    my deliverer;
The God of my strength, in whom I will
    trust;
My shield and the horn of my salvation,
My stronghold and my refuge.

2 SAMUEL 22:2–3

You reign over all.
In Your hand is power and might;
In Your hand it is to make great
And to give strength to all.

1 CHRONICLES 29: 12

*Father, thank You for providing me with
Your strength whenever I ask. Thank You
for giving me the strength to love You, to
obey Your commands, and to navigate
life's challenges in every season. Amen.*

25

God's Gift of Worship

We reflect the humility of Jesus, the Suffering Servant and our Savior, when we come before the Lord on our knees in worship, praise, and repentance. Our physical posture reflects hearts humbled by the boundless mercy and grace of our heavenly Father; our kneeling indicates hearts yielded to His will for our lives and open to His guidance. Kneeling before the Almighty honors Him and—equally as important if not more so—reminds us that He is God and we are not. We truly do stand tallest when we are on our knees before our Lord and King.

Oh come, let us sing to the Lord!
Let us shout joyfully to the Rock of our
        salvation.
Let us come before His presence with
        thanksgiving;
Let us shout joyfully to Him with psalms.
For the Lord is the great God,
And the great King above all gods. . . .
Oh come, let us worship and bow down;
Let us kneel before the Lord our Maker.
For He is our God,
And we are the people of His pasture,
And the sheep of His hand.

PSALM 95:1–3, 6–7

Give unto the Lord, O you mighty ones,
Give unto the Lord glory and strength.
Give unto the Lord the glory due to
        His name;
Worship the Lord in the beauty of
        holiness.

PSALM 29:1–2

Give to the Lord the glory due His name;
Bring an offering, and come into His
courts.
Oh, worship the Lord in the beauty of
holiness!
Tremble before Him, all the earth.
Say among the nations, "The Lord reigns;
The world also is firmly established,
It shall not be moved;
He shall judge the peoples righteously."

PSALM 96:8–10

I was glad when they said to me,
"Let us go into the house of the Lord."

PSALM 122:1

It is good to give thanks to the Lord,
And to sing praises to Your name, O
Most High;
To declare Your lovingkindness in the
morning,
And Your faithfulness every night.

PSALM 92:1–2

Kneeling, Lord, I worship You with gratitude, humbly seeking forgiveness for my sins, marveling at Your grace, listening for Your guidance, and asking You to use me in Your kingdom work now and always. Amen.

26

GOD'S GIFT OF SIGNIFICANCE

The Lord proclaimed, "My thoughts are not your thoughts; nor are your ways My ways" (Isaiah 55:8). No wonder we may be baffled by why He chooses the least, the weakest, the easily overlooked and discounted in the world. We may be baffled by why He chose us. And He chose us simply because He loves us (Deuteronomy 7:8). Being loved by the Almighty is reason enough to stand tall and walk boldly into the future. He will guide your decisions, answer when you pray, and bless the ways you serve Him. You and your life are significant to Him.

"Fear not, for I have redeemed you;
I have called you by your name;
You are Mine.
When you pass through the waters, I will
        be with you;
And through the rivers, they shall not
        overflow you.
When you walk through the fire, you shall
        not be burned,
Nor shall the flame scorch you.
For I am the LORD your God,
The Holy One of Israel, your Savior."

ISAIAH 43:1–3

"Let the little children come to Me, and do not forbid them; for of such is the kingdom of God. Assuredly, I say to you, whoever does not receive the kingdom of God as a little child will by no means enter it."

MARK 10:14–15

I know the thoughts that I think toward you, says the LORD, thoughts of peace and not of evil, to give you a future and a hope.

JEREMIAH 29:11

Not many wise according to the flesh, not many mighty, not many noble, are called. But God has chosen the foolish things of the world to put to shame the wise, and God has chosen the weak things of the world to put to shame the things which are mighty.

1 CORINTHIANS 1:26–27

You are a holy people to the LORD your God; the LORD your God has chosen you to be a people for Himself, a special treasure above all the peoples on the face of the earth. The LORD did not set His love on you nor choose you because you were more in number than any other people, for you were the least of all peoples; but because the LORD loves you.

DEUTERONOMY 7:6–8

*Lord, guide my life so it may be
significant in that it honors You.
Humbled by Your love, I want to hear
at the end my life Your "Well done,
good and faithful servant." Amen.*

27

GOD'S GIFT OF FRIENDSHIP

As you graduate and venture into a new chapter of life, you will meet many people. Choose wisely those whom you befriend. After all, our friends can have a huge influence on us, either for good or for bad. Ideally, like-minded followers of Jesus will be your closest friends for life. Yet always be mindful of that Friend of yours who sticks closer than a brother. Walking through life with Jesus will mean peace, joy, and fulfillment beyond what you can imagine. What a eulogy that would be: "[Your name] was a friend of Jesus."

When Moses entered the tabernacle . . . the pillar of cloud descended and stood at the door of the tabernacle, and the LORD talked with Moses. All the people saw the pillar of cloud standing at the tabernacle door, and all the people rose and worshiped, each man in his tent door. So the LORD spoke to Moses face to face, as a man speaks to his friend.

EXODUS 33:9–11

A man who has friends must himself be
friendly,
But there is a friend who sticks closer
than a brother.

PROVERBS 18:24

The soul of Jonathan was knit to the soul of David, and Jonathan loved him as his own soul.

1 SAMUEL 18:1

"Abraham believed God, and it was accounted to him for righteousness." And he was called the friend of God.

JAMES 2:23

"This is My commandment, that you love one another as I have loved you. Greater love has no one than this, than to lay down one's life for his friends. You are My friends if you do whatever I command you. No longer do I call you servants, for a servant does not know what his master is doing; but I have called you friends, for all things that I heard from My Father I have made known to you."

JOHN 15:12–15

Father, help me be a good friend who reflects in my words and actions my ultimate friendship with Jesus. Enable me to love with His love and to be a blessing to people along my path. Amen.

28

GOD'S GIFT OF PURPOSE

As you've thought about venturing forth after graduation, have you considered what God's purpose is for your life? Have you asked Him what He wants you to do with the personality, skills, talents, education, and experience He has blessed you with? God will use you for His glory whatever His path for you is, and He will reveal that plan, as well as the path, when you open your heart to His leading. Simply by surrendering your life to God, you open the door to a life of purpose that glorifies Him in all you say and do.

He has shown you, O man, what is good;
And what does the Lord require of you
But to do justly,
To love mercy,
And to walk humbly with your God?

MICAH 6:8

"'You shall love the Lord your God with all your heart, with all your soul, and with all your mind.' This is the first and great commandment. And the second is like it: 'You shall love your neighbor as yourself.'"

MATTHEW 22:37–39

"Now My soul is troubled, and what shall I say? 'Father, save Me from this hour'? But for this purpose I came to this hour. Father, glorify Your name."

JOHN 12:27–28

Whether you eat or drink, or whatever you do, do all to the glory of God.

1 CORINTHIANS 10:31

The LORD said to Moses, "Rise early in the morning and stand before Pharaoh, and say to him, 'Thus says the LORD God of the Hebrews: "Let My people go, that they may serve Me, for at this time I will send all My plagues to your very heart, and on your servants and on your people, that you may know that there is none like Me in all the earth. . . . But indeed for this purpose I have raised you up, that I may show My power in you, and that My name may be declared in all the earth.'"

EXODUS 9:13–14, 16

Father, may my path in life clearly reflect Your purpose for my life. As You guide my steps, I ask You to help me serve for Your glory and love with Your love. Amen.

29

GOD'S GIFT OF ARMOR
FOR THE BATTLE

God has given us His armor, a clear acknowledgment that you and I are in a war. We are battling the Enemy's darkness and deceit, the world that discounts our Christian faith, and the relentless pressure to sin, to choose our way instead of God's way. The armor God provides us is composed of His truth; His righteousness; the gospel message; faith in Him; salvation from eternal condemnation for our sins; and His Word of instruction, grace, and hope. By God's grace, this armor enables us to withstand the evil of the twenty-first-century world in which we live.

Be strong in the Lord and in the power of His might. Put on the whole armor of God, that you may be able to stand against the wiles of the devil. For we do not wrestle against flesh and blood, but against principalities, against powers, against the rulers of the darkness of this age, against spiritual hosts of wickedness in the heavenly places. Therefore take up the whole armor of God, that you may be able to withstand in the evil day, and having done all, to stand.

EPHESIANS 6:10–13

Stand therefore, having girded your waist with truth, having put on the breastplate of righteousness, and having shod your feet with the preparation of the gospel of peace; above all, taking the shield of faith with which you will be able to quench all the fiery darts of the wicked one. And take the helmet of salvation, and the sword of the Spirit, which is the word of God; praying always with all prayer and supplication in the Spirit.

EPHESIANS 6:14–18

Let all those rejoice who put their trust in
     You;
Let them ever shout for joy, because You
     defend them;
Let those also who love Your name
Be joyful in You.
For You, O Lord, will bless the righteous;
With favor You will surround him as with
     a shield.

PSALM 5:11–12

Our salvation is nearer than when we first believed. The night is far spent, the day is at hand. Therefore let us cast off the works of darkness, and let us put on the armor of light. Let us walk properly, as in the day, not in revelry and drunkenness, not in lewdness and lust, not in strife and envy. But put on the Lord Jesus Christ, and make no provision for the flesh, to fulfill its lusts.

ROMANS 13:11–14

Every word of God is pure;
He is a shield to those who put their trust
in Him.

PROVERBS 30:5

Father, You enabled Your Son to emerge victorious in His battle against sin and death. Thank You for armor that will help me effectively fight the battle against the darkness of this present day. Amen.

3 0

GOD'S GIFT OF WISDOM

When he reigned and still today, King Solomon has been known for his wisdom, and that God-given wisdom is available to all of us. As James wrote, we simply need to ask for it. The Holy Spirit can help us learn the wisdom of the Bible: Scripture teaches us what to do and what to avoid. We can also ask the Spirit to give us not only wisdom for specific circumstances and decisions we face but also help in living it out. As wise people know, God's way is the best way to live in every season and chapter of life.

The LORD gives wisdom;
From His mouth come knowledge and
understanding.

PROVERBS 2:6

"Whoever hears these sayings of Mine, and does them, I will liken him to a wise man who built his house on the rock: and the rain descended, the floods came, and the winds blew and beat on that house; and it did not fall, for it was founded on the rock."

MATTHEW 7:24–25

Oh, how I love Your law!
It is my meditation all the day.
You, through Your commandments, make
me wiser than my enemies.

PSALM 119:97–98

If any of you lacks wisdom, let him ask of God, who gives to all liberally and without reproach, and it will be given to him.

JAMES 1:5

Happy is the man who finds wisdom,
And the man who gains understanding;
For her proceeds are better than the
    profits of silver,
And her gain than fine gold.
She is more precious than rubies,
And all the things you may desire cannot
    compare with her. . . .
She is a tree of life to those who take hold
    of her,
And happy are all who retain her.

PROVERBS 3:13–15, 18

Heavenly Father, please grant me Your wisdom. Holy Spirit, enable me to live according to it. Help my life always reflect my knowledge of both Your written Word—the Bible—and Your living Word, Jesus. Amen.

31

GOD'S GIFT OF HIS BLESSING

God is love, so of course He loves to bless His people. He blesses us in myriad ways, and He always blesses us so we will be able to bless others. As wounded healers, forgiven saints, and fellow pilgrims, we can offer one another support and encouragement. As you begin this next chapter of your life, seek out people who can come alongside you and bless you with their knowledge and experience. At the same time be aware of people you can come alongside to encourage and support in some way. Blessed to be a blessing is God's way.

Now the Lord had said to Abram:

"Get out of your country,
From your family
And from your father's house,
To a land that I will show you.
I will make you a great nation;
I will bless you
And make your name great;
And you shall be a blessing.
I will bless those who bless you,
And I will curse him who curses you;
And in you all the families of the earth
shall be blessed."

GENESIS 12:1–3

He who has clean hands and a pure heart,
Who has not lifted up his soul to an idol,
Nor sworn deceitfully.
He shall receive blessing from the Lord,
And righteousness from the God of his
salvation.

PSALM 24:4–5

The LORD spoke to Moses, saying: "Speak to Aaron and his sons, saying, 'This is the way you shall bless the children of Israel. Say to them:

"The LORD bless you and keep you;
The LORD make His face shine upon you,
And be gracious to you;
The LORD lift up His countenance
    upon you,
And give you peace."'

"So they shall put My name on the children of Israel, and I will bless them."

NUMBERS 6:22–27

"Blessed are the poor in spirit,
For theirs is the kingdom of heaven.
Blessed are those who mourn,
For they shall be comforted.
Blessed are the meek,
For they shall inherit the earth.
Blessed are those who hunger and thirst
    for righteousness,

For they shall be filled.
Blessed are the merciful,
For they shall obtain mercy.
Blessed are the pure in heart,
For they shall see God.
Blessed are the peacemakers,
For they shall be called sons of God.
Blessed are those who are persecuted for
    righteousness' sake,
For theirs is the kingdom of heaven."

MATTHEW 5:3–10

Blessed is every one who fears the Lord,
Who walks in His ways.

PSALM 128:1

Lord, I am humbled by and grateful
for Your goodness to me. Thank You
for blessing me abundantly every day.
Please use me to be a light in this world
and a blessing to others. Amen.

32

GOD'S GIFT OF JOY

In this next season of life and beyond, God wants you to know joy. In fact, His gift of the Holy Spirit's presence with and within you brings joy. God also gives each of us many unique and personal reasons for joy. (I find joy in a crackling fire, a good book, homemade bread, grandkids, longtime friendships, and songs of worship.) Joy, however, is also a choice: Will you look to Jesus and see in Him forgiveness and the promise of a joy-filled eternity—or will you choose worry, depression, anger, bitterness, or fear? Receive joy! Choose joy!

The fruit of the Spirit is love, joy, peace, longsuffering, kindness, goodness, faithfulness, gentleness, self-control.

GALATIANS 5:22–23

In Your presence is fullness of joy.

PSALM 16:11

My soul shall be joyful in the LORD;
It shall rejoice in His salvation.

PSALM 35:9

"These [commandments and instructions] I have spoken to you, that My joy may remain in you, and that your joy may be full."

JOHN 15:11

May the God of hope fill you with all joy and peace in believing, that you may abound in hope by the power of the Holy Spirit.

ROMANS 15:13

Father, thank You for the gift of joy.
Please help me both to choose joy
whatever my circumstances and then
to explain to anyone who asks the
gospel reason for my joy. Amen.

33

GOD'S GIFT OF ENCOURAGEMENT

At one time or another, we all need someone to put courage into us, someone to
*en*courage us. God does exactly that through
the promises and truths in His Word. Wherever
life takes you, take God's Word with you. Open
its pages when you're discouraged, confused,
or exhausted. Let the Holy Spirit use God's living Word to breathe courage into you. Also be
willing to be an encourager to others. You shine
God's light when you offer support or a listening
ear. Sharing the gift of encouragement is a great
way to love others the way God has loved you.

"In the world you will have tribulation; but be of good cheer, I have overcome the world."

JOHN 16:33

If God is for us, who can be against us?

ROMANS 8:31

Let us consider one another in order to stir up love and good works, not forsaking the assembling of ourselves together.

HEBREWS 10:24–25

"Be strong and of good courage; do not be afraid, nor be dismayed, for the LORD your God is with you wherever you go."

JOSHUA 1:9

Blessed be the God and Father of our Lord Jesus Christ, the Father of mercies and God of all comfort, who comforts us in all our tribulation, that we may be able to comfort those who are in any trouble, with the comfort with which we ourselves are comforted by God.

2 CORINTHIANS 1:3–4

Lord, thank You for being a faithful encourager. I know You will continue to encourage me in this new season. Just as You have lifted me up, please use me to inspire others. Amen.

34

GOD'S GIFT OF
RIGHTEOUSNESS

God is holy, we are not, and the result is a chasm between Him and us that we human beings can't bridge. But we don't have to because God has provided that bridge, the one and only way for us to be in right standing with Him. According to Scripture, we attain the righteousness of God when we turn from our sin and put our faith in Jesus Christ. Because of Jesus' sacrificial death and His resurrection, we can know God's forgiveness. He declares us righteous and welcomes us into relationship with Himself. May that relationship sustain you throughout your life.

Now the righteousness of God apart from the law is revealed . . . through faith in Jesus Christ, to all and on all who believe.

ROMANS 3:21–22

[The LORD] brought [Abram] outside and said, "Look now toward heaven, and count the stars if you are able to number them." And He said to him, "So shall your descendants be."

And [Abram] believed in the LORD, and He accounted it to him for righteousness.

GENESIS 15:4–6

To him who . . . believes on Him who justifies the ungodly, his faith is accounted for righteousness.

ROMANS 4:5

With the heart one believes unto righteousness, and with the mouth confession is made unto salvation.

ROMANS 10:10

[God] made [Jesus] who knew no sin to be sin for us, that we might become the righteousness of God in Him.

2 CORINTHIANS 5:21

Jesus, thank You for taking on my unrighteousness and dying on the cross so I might be credited with Your righteousness. May I honor that great sacrifice and gift each day of my life. Amen.

35

GOD'S GIFT OF THE GOSPEL

Perhaps the best-known Bible verse, John 3:16 offers a concise statement of the gospel. That word *gospel* means "good news," and this verse's declaration of God's love is indeed good news. This verse sets forth the surprisingly simple but completely transformative truth that naming God's "only begotten Son" as your Savior means eternal life. Upon accepting this truth, we are to respond to Jesus' commission: "Go therefore and make disciples of all the nations" (Matthew 28:19). This sharing of the gospel is both a privilege and a responsibility. Look for opportunities to share the gift of God's gospel love.

God so loved the world that He gave His only begotten Son, that whoever believes in Him should not perish but have everlasting life. For God did not send His Son into the world to condemn the world, but that the world through Him might be saved.

JOHN 3:16–17

Blessed be the God and Father of our Lord Jesus Christ, who according to His abundant mercy has begotten us again to a living hope through the resurrection of Jesus Christ from the dead, to an inheritance incorruptible and undefiled and that does not fade away, reserved in heaven for you, who are kept by the power of God through faith for salvation ready to be revealed in the last time.

1 PETER 1:3–5

Worthy is the Lamb who was slain
    To receive power and riches and wisdom,
    And strength and honor and glory and blessing!

REVELATION 5:12

As through one man's offense judgment came to all men, resulting in condemnation, even so through one Man's righteous act the free gift came to all men, resulting in justification of life. For as by one man's disobedience many were made sinners, so also by one Man's obedience many will be made righteous.

ROMANS 5:18–19

[Christ Jesus] made Himself of no reputation, taking the form of a bondservant, and coming in the likeness of men. And being found in appearance as a man, He humbled Himself and became obedient to the point of death, even the death of the cross. Therefore God also has highly exalted Him and given Him the name which is above every name, that at the name of Jesus every knee should bow, of those in heaven, and of those on earth, and of those under the earth, and that every tongue should confess that Jesus Christ is Lord, to the glory of God the Father.

PHILIPPIANS 2:7–11

Lord, whatever career I pursue and whatever path I travel, may I also be faithful to proclaim with my actions as well as my words the good news of salvation through faith in Jesus. Amen.

36

GOD'S GIFT OF PRAYER

It's easy to approach the gift of prayer as a "have-to" rather than a privilege and joy. Yet prayer is the incredible freedom to communicate with our heavenly and holy Father about anything and everything as we share our heart and hurts, as we lift before Him people we love and circumstances we encounter, and as we seek His wisdom and guidance. The Bible records God's faithful responses to hundreds of prayers as well as encouragement to pray and the teaching that Jesus Himself and the Holy Spirit pray for us. May we find joy when we pray to God.

We have a great High Priest who has passed through the heavens, Jesus the Son of God. . . . Let us therefore come boldly to the throne of grace, that we may obtain mercy and find grace to help in time of need.

HEBREWS 4:14, 16

We do not know what we should pray for as we ought, but the Spirit Himself makes intercession for us with groanings which cannot be uttered. Now He who searches the hearts knows what the mind of the Spirit is, because He makes intercession for the saints according to the will of God.

ROMANS 8:26–27

This is the confidence that we have in Him, that if we ask anything according to His will, He hears us. And if we know that He hears us, whatever we ask, we know that we have the petitions that we have asked of Him.

1 JOHN 5:14–15

Christ who died, and furthermore is also risen . . . is even at the right hand of God, who also makes intercession for us.

ROMANS 8:34

Rejoice always, pray without ceasing, in everything give thanks; for this is the will of God in Christ Jesus for you.

1 THESSALONIANS 5:16–18

Holy God, what a privilege to be able to come before You in prayer 24–7! And what a blessing to have Jesus and the Spirit praying for me! I am humbled and grateful. I love You. Amen.

37

GOD'S GIFT OF RESTORATION

Beauty for ashes—perhaps that's the best three-word definition of *restoration* or *redemption*. When we choose sin over obedient devotion to God, when we human beings pursue our own goals and worldly success instead of God's will, and when we are careless and hurtful in relationships, we need restoration. God grants that grace when we confess our sins, when we ask forgiveness, and when we return to seeking after His will. The ashes we have made in our lives become beautiful as He redeems them and transforms us. Praise God for His restorative love and redemptive powers!

"When he was still a great way off, his father saw him and had compassion, and ran and fell on his neck and kissed him. And the son said to him, 'Father, I have sinned against heaven and in your sight, and am no longer worthy to be called your son.'

"But the father said to his servants, 'Bring out the best robe and put it on him, and put a ring on his hand and sandals on his feet. And bring the fatted calf here and kill it, and let us eat and be merry; for this my son was dead and is alive again; he was lost and is found.' And they began to be merry."

LUKE 15:20–24

[The good Shepherd] restores my soul.

PSALM 23:3

Restore us, O God of hosts;
Cause Your face to shine,
And we shall be saved!

PSALM 80:7

The Spirit of the Lord God is upon Me,
Because the Lord has anointed Me . . .
To heal the brokenhearted,
To proclaim liberty to the captives,
And the opening of the prison to those
      who are bound . . .
To comfort all who mourn . . .
To give them beauty for ashes,
The oil of joy for mourning,
The garment of praise for the spirit of
      heaviness.

ISAIAH 61:1–3

"I will restore to you the years that the swarming locust has eaten."

JOEL 2:25

Lord, You know where I need Your restorative touch and redemptive power in my heart, my life, and my relationships. Thank You in advance for giving me beauty for ashes. Amen.

38

GOD'S GIFT OF HIS WORD

In every season of life, God's Word helps us know Him better and understand more clearly how we are to live. We can learn lessons from our forerunners in the faith, from their shining moments as well as their missteps. We see God's plan for our salvation and read about His ultimate victory over Satan and sin. We recognize not only our sin but also the grace and goodness of our unchanging God in dealing with us. Studying God's Word clarifies our path and, by the power of God's Spirit, transforms our hearts. May we always faithfully study God's life-giving Word.

All Scripture is given by inspiration of God, and is profitable for doctrine, for reproof, for correction, for instruction in righteousness, that the man of God may be complete, thoroughly equipped for every good work.

2 TIMOTHY 3:16–17

Your word is a lamp to my feet
And a light to my path.

PSALM 119:105

Let the word of Christ dwell in you richly in all wisdom, teaching and admonishing one another in psalms and hymns and spiritual songs, singing with grace in your hearts to the Lord.

COLOSSIANS 3:16

My son, do not forget my law,
But let your heart keep my commands. . . .
Let not mercy and truth forsake you;
Bind them around your neck,
Write them on the tablet of your heart.

PROVERBS 3:1, 3

The law of the LORD is perfect, converting
the soul;
The testimony of the LORD is sure, making
wise the simple;
The statutes of the LORD are right,
rejoicing the heart;
The commandment of the LORD is pure,
enlightening the eyes;
The fear of the LORD is clean, enduring
forever;
The judgments of the LORD are true and
righteous altogether.
More to be desired are they than gold,
Yea, than much fine gold;
Sweeter also than honey and the
honeycomb.
Moreover by them Your servant is
warned,
And in keeping them there is great
reward.

PSALM 19:7–11

Lord, Your written Word is an invaluable gift, providing me truth, wisdom, direction, history, commandments, beauty, encouragement, conviction, hope, and joy. Please give me a hunger for Your Word and joy in studying it. Amen.

39

GOD'S GIFT OF HIS PRESENCE

An Old Testament name for God is *Emmanuel,* "God with us." This gift of His presence reveals His desire to be involved in our daily lives. He waits for us to choose to walk with Him, to ask Him for wisdom, and to seek His will. Imagine living your day-to-day life with the awareness of God's presence with you and, because of the Holy Spirit, His power within you. What specific steps will you take to live more aware of God's presence with you? That awareness will mean living in His power according to His wisdom and with greater joy.

[The Lord] is not far from each one of us; for in Him we live and move and have our being.

ACTS 17:27–28

In Your presence is fullness of joy;
At Your right hand are pleasures
    forevermore.

PSALM 16:11

Where can I go from Your Spirit?
Or where can I flee from Your presence?

PSALM 139:7

"Fear not, for I am with you;
Be not dismayed, for I am your God.
I will strengthen you,
Yes, I will help you,
I will uphold you with My righteous
    right hand."

ISAIAH 41:10

"I am with you always, even to the end of the age."

MATTHEW 28:20

Lord, I am well aware of my shortcomings, lack of wisdom, and sinfulness. I need You. Please help me to live with a sharper awareness of Your loving and faithful presence in my life. Amen.

40

GOD'S GIFT OF BOUNDARIES

When a friend follows through on a promise, we feel valued and respected. Similarly, God the Father is honored when those of us whom He has adopted as His children live within the boundaries He has set for us (1 John 3:1). When we choose to align our actions with God's commands, when we choose to yield to the boundaries He has established for our good, we know the blessing of His pleasure in us and the peace that comes with honoring Him. You'll know God's blessings as you make obeying Him your priority in every season of life.

"You are My friends if you do whatever I command you."

This is love, that we walk according to His commandments. This is the commandment [that we love one another], that as you have heard from the beginning, you should walk in it.

2 JOHN 1:6

"Blessed are those who hear the word of God and keep it!"

LUKE 11:28

Be doers of the word, and not hearers only, deceiving yourselves.

JAMES 1:22

[Bring] every thought into captivity to the obedience of Christ.

2 CORINTHIANS 10:5

Lord, thank You for showing me that I can honor You with my actions. May I also show You my love by choosing to respect the boundaries You have set for my thoughts, words, and actions. Amen.

41

GOD'S GIFT OF DELIVERANCE FROM DARK MOMENTS

Dark moments and even dark seasons come along in life. The best preparation is learning God's Word and getting to know Him well before those inevitable times come. Then, when they do, remember the truth of today's passages that testify to God's capable deliverance of His people. He can and does rescue His children from whatever darkness surrounds and suffocates us. When the darkness of hard times, pain, loss, struggle, and stress keep you from praising God and testifying to His saving goodness, cry out to God and receive His love. He will bring light into your darkness.

I sought the LORD, and He heard me,
And delivered me from all my fears.

PSALM 34:4

The righteous cry out, and the LORD hears,
And delivers them out of all their troubles.

PSALM 34:17

[The redeemed] cried out to the LORD in
their trouble,
And He delivered them out of their
distresses.

PSALM 107:6

The LORD is my rock and my fortress and
my deliverer;
The God of my strength, in whom I will
trust;
My shield and the horn of my salvation,
My stronghold and my refuge;
My Savior, You save me from violence.
I will call upon the LORD, who is worthy to
be praised;
So shall I be saved from my enemies.

2 SAMUEL 22:2–4

I waited patiently for the LORD;
And He inclined to me,
And heard my cry.
He also brought me up out of a
		horrible pit,
Out of the miry clay,
And set my feet upon a rock,
And established my steps.
He has put a new song in my mouth—
Praise to our God;
Many will see it and fear,
And will trust in the LORD.

PSALM 40:1–3

Holy Spirit, when I encounter dark seasons, please prompt me right away to cry out instead of sitting and sinking deeper. May I quickly turn to You and live once again in Your light. Amen.

42

GOD'S GIFT OF
SPIRITUAL GROWTH

Whether we're talking about botany or our soul, growth requires light, nutrition, and attention. To grow spiritually, we need to spend time in God's light, time praying, worshiping, and reading and studying Scripture. These actions simultaneously feed our spirit and soul with God's truth—written, spoken, and sung. So does spending time listening for His voice. With every step we take to get the light and nutrition we need, we are tending to our spiritual growth, to uninvited weeds, to lack of sunshine, and to inadequate nourishment. The Lord—who wants you to grow—will help you in the process.

We should no longer be children, tossed to and fro and carried about with every wind of doctrine, by the trickery of men, in the cunning craftiness of deceitful plotting, but, speaking the truth in love, may grow up in all things into Him who is the head—Christ.

EPHESIANS 4:14–15

Add to your faith virtue, to virtue knowledge, to knowledge self-control, to self-control perseverance, to perseverance godliness, to godliness brotherly kindness, and to brotherly kindness love. For if these things are yours and abound, you will be neither barren nor unfruit-ful in the knowledge of our Lord Jesus Christ.

2 PETER 1:5–8

Put off, concerning your former conduct, the old man which grows corrupt according to the deceitful lusts, and be renewed in the spirit of your mind, and that you put on the new man which was created according to God, in true righteousness and holiness.

EPHESIANS 4:22–24

Blessed is the man
Who walks not in the counsel of the
    ungodly,
Nor stands in the path of sinners,
Nor sits in the seat of the scornful;
But his delight is in the law of the LORD,
And in His law he meditates day and
    night.
He shall be like a tree
Planted by the rivers of water,
That brings forth its fruit in its season,
Whose leaf also shall not wither;
And whatever he does shall prosper.

PSALM 1:1–3

We . . . ask that you may be filled with the knowledge of His will in all wisdom and spiritual understanding; that you may walk worthy of the Lord, fully pleasing Him, being fruitful in every good work and increasing in the knowledge of God; strengthened with all might, according to His glorious power, for all patience and longsuffering with joy.

COLOSSIANS 1:9–11

*Lord, in this new chapter and always,
help me attend to the important, not
merely the urgent. Help me make spiritual
growth and time with You a priority
whatever the demands of life. Amen.*

43

GOD'S GIFT OF HIS
TRUSTWORTHINESS

Why do we struggle to trust our completely trustworthy God? The Bible presents proof through the millennia of His great faithfulness to His people. The history of the church and the lives of our fellow believers offer the same. Our own lives offer rich evidence of His trustworthiness if we are able to remember those times when our worries mounted. And graduation may be sparking worries. This momentous occasion does invite dependence on the Lord to perhaps a new degree. Rather than worrying about the future, make the deliberate choice to put your life in the hands of Your trustworthy God.

The LORD also will be a refuge for the
        oppressed,
A refuge in times of trouble.
And those who know Your name will put
        their trust in You;
For You, LORD, have not forsaken those
        who seek You.

PSALM 9:9–10

I sought the LORD, and He heard me,
And delivered me from all my fears.
They looked to Him and were radiant,
And their faces were not ashamed.
This poor man cried out, and the LORD
        heard him,
And saved him out of all his troubles.
The angel of the LORD encamps all around
        those who fear Him,
And delivers them.
Oh, taste and see that the LORD is good;
Blessed is the man who trusts in Him!

PSALM 34:4–8

He who calls you is faithful, who also will do it.

1 THESSALONIANS 5:24

Commit your way to the LORD,

Trust also in Him,

And He shall bring it to pass.

He shall bring forth your righteousness as
the light,

And your justice as the noonday.

PSALM 37:5-6

Know that the LORD your God, He is God, the
faithful God who keeps covenant and mercy
for a thousand generations with those who love
Him and keep His commandments.

DEUTERONOMY 7:9

*Lord, You are worthy of my complete
trust, yet I easily doubt. Help me
remember Your faithfulness to me in
the past, that I may wholly trust You in
the present and for the future. Amen.*

44

GOD'S GIFT OF WAITING ON HIM

Waiting rarely feels like a gift, yet God does some good work when we wait *on* Him and when we wait *with* Him. When we wait *on* Him for instructions, choosing to act only when He reveals His plan, we avoid missteps and pitfalls. When we wait *with* Him, He grows our relationship with Him, our trust in Him, and our sensitivity to His presence. Consider how the Almighty grew Moses, Joseph, and David as they waited *on* Him and *with* Him for His purposes to unfold. At this crossroads in your life, wait *on* God and wait *with* Him.

I wait for the Lord, my soul waits,
And in His word I do hope.
My soul waits for the Lord
More than those who watch for the
        morning—
Yes, more than those who watch for the
        morning.

PSALM 130:5–6

Blessed is the man who listens to me,
Watching daily at my gates,
Waiting at the posts of my doors.
For whoever finds me finds life,
And obtains favor from the Lord.

PROVERBS 8:34–35

Wait on the Lord;
Be of good courage,
And He shall strengthen your heart;
Wait, I say, on the Lord!

PSALM 27:14

The Lord is good to those who wait for
     Him,
To the soul who seeks Him.
It is good that one should hope and wait
     quietly
For the salvation of the Lord.

LAMENTATIONS 3:25–26

My soul, wait silently for God alone,
For my expectation is from Him.
He only is my rock and my salvation;
He is my defense;
I shall not be moved.

PSALM 62:5–6

Lord, You know how ready I am for plans for this next season to fall into place. But I want to wait on You and wait with You as Your plans for me unfold. Amen.

45

GOD'S GIFT OF
TESTS AND TRIALS

Jesus promised that we would face trials (John 16:33), but He also promised that He would be with us always (Matthew 28:20). During those tribulations and tests, Jesus may seem far away and silent. We may wonder what we're supposed to learn in the darkness and pain. But when His light breaks through, we'll see that our faith has been strengthened, that He revealed His love by sustaining us, and that we have gained some insight into Jesus' sufferings and greater anticipation of the kingdom glory that awaits us. Know that God doesn't send the pain; neither does He waste it.

My brethren, count it all joy when you fall into various trials, knowing that the testing of your faith produces patience. But let patience have its perfect work, that you may be perfect and complete, lacking nothing.

JAMES 1:2–4

In this you greatly rejoice, though now for a little while, if need be, you have been grieved by various trials, that the genuineness of your faith, being much more precious than gold that perishes, though it is tested by fire, may be found to praise, honor, and glory at the revelation of Jesus Christ.

1 PETER 1:6–7

May the God of all grace, who called us to His eternal glory by Christ Jesus, after you have suffered a while, perfect, establish, strengthen, and settle you.

1 PETER 5:10

No temptation has overtaken you except such as is common to man; but God is faithful, who will not allow you to be tempted beyond what you are able, but with the temptation will also make the way of escape, that you may be able to bear it.

I CORINTHIANS 10:13

Who shall separate us from the love of Christ? Shall tribulation, or distress, or persecution, or famine, or nakedness, or peril, or sword?

ROMANS 8:35

Lord, I know that I will face various tests and trials on any path of life I walk. Help me know Your strength and peace so that You can use the pain to refine my faith. Amen.

46

GOD'S GIFT OF ABIDING IN HIM

So what exactly does *abide* even mean? *Merriam-Webster's* offers this: "to remain stable" and "to continue in a place." No better place *to remain stable* exists—no better place *to continue in* exists—than the presence of God! And what amazing blessings come with that abiding! When we abide in God, we can know His love, we are able to share His love, we bear fruit for His kingdom, God's Word abides in us, and, Scripture says, God Himself abides in us (1 John 4:16). May abiding in the Almighty be your top priority whatever season of life you're in.

"I am the true vine, and My Father is the vinedresser. Every branch in Me that does not bear fruit He takes away; and every branch that bears fruit He prunes, that it may bear more fruit. . . . Abide in Me, and I in you. As the branch cannot bear fruit of itself, unless it abides in the vine, neither can you, unless you abide in Me."

JOHN 15:1–2, 4

"I am the vine, you are the branches. He who abides in Me, and I in him, bears much fruit; for without Me you can do nothing. If anyone does not abide in Me, he is cast out as a branch and is withered; and they gather them and throw them into the fire, and they are burned. If you abide in Me, and My words abide in you, you will ask what you desire, and it shall be done for you. By this My Father is glorified, that you bear much fruit; so you will be My disciples."

JOHN 15:5–8

If we love one another, God abides in us. . . . By this we know that we abide in Him, and He in us, because He has given us of His Spirit. And we have seen and testify that the Father has sent the Son as Savior of the world.

1 JOHN 4:12–14

Whoever confesses that Jesus is the Son of God, God abides in him, and he in God. And we have known and believed the love that God has for us. God is love, and he who abides in love abides in God, and God in him.

1 JOHN 4:15–16

Whoever transgresses and does not abide in the doctrine of Christ does not have God. He who abides in the doctrine of Christ has both the Father and the Son.

2 JOHN 1:9

Lord, help me abide in You whatever the demands of life and whatever decisions weigh on me. I know I need time with You if I'm to honor You as this next chapter unfolds, and always. Amen.

47

GOD'S GIFT OF COMPANIONSHIP

Graciously, our God is present with each of His children 24–7. Also graciously, He gives us each other, a blessing that brings blessings. Fellow believers support us, listen to us, and pray for us. When they cry with us, they help us bear the sadness. When they celebrate with us, they increase our joy. In Christian community we strengthen one another's faith, enabling us to shine the light of Jesus more brightly in the world and to more effectively serve as Jesus Himself served. May we never let ourselves get too busy to invest in relationships and build Christian community.

Two are better than one,

Because they have a good reward for
their labor.

For if they fall, one will lift up his
companion.

But woe to him who is alone when he
falls,

For he has no one to help him up.

Again, if two lie down together, they will
keep warm;

But how can one be warm alone?

Though one may be overpowered by
another, two can withstand him.

And a threefold cord is not quickly
broken.

ECCLESIASTES 4:9–12

The LORD God said, "It is not good that man
should be alone; I will make him a helper com-
parable to him." . . .

And the LORD God caused a deep sleep to
fall on Adam, and he slept; and He took one of
his ribs, and closed up the flesh in its place.

GENESIS 2:18, 21

Continuing daily with one accord in the temple, and breaking bread from house to house, they ate their food with gladness and simplicity of heart, praising God and having favor with all the people. And the Lord added to the church daily those who were being saved.

ACTS 2:46–47

If there is any consolation in Christ, if any comfort of love, if any fellowship of the Spirit, if any affection and mercy, fulfill my joy by being like-minded, having the same love, being of one accord, of one mind. Let nothing be done through selfish ambition or conceit, but in lowliness of mind let each esteem others better than himself. Let each of you look out not only for his own interests, but also for the interests of others.

PHILIPPIANS 2:1–4

Now the multitude of those who believed were of one heart and one soul; neither did anyone say that any of the things he possessed was his own, but they had all things in common. And with great power the apostles gave witness to the resurrection of the Lord Jesus. And great grace was upon them all.

ACTS 4:32–33

Lord, thank You for the family of fellow believers. Convict me if I ever fail to keep gathering with brothers and sisters in Christ. I want to live according to Your design of Christian community. Amen.

48

GOD'S GIFT OF HIS
PROMISED RETURN

During His earthly ministry that culminated in His death and resurrection, Jesus told His followers that He would one day return as conquering King. As we, Jesus' twenty-first-century followers, still await that return, we find comfort and hope in His promises as well as in details about His judgment of unbelievers, His rewards for His people, and His eternal reign on the new earth. Jesus will prove victorious over sin and Satan and death. And our good God has for us an eternity free of pain and tears. No wonder John ended the book of Revelation with "Come, Lord Jesus!" (22:20).

The Lord Himself will descend from heaven with a shout, with the voice of an archangel, and with the trumpet of God. And the dead in Christ will rise first. Then we who are alive and remain shall be caught up together with them in the clouds to meet the Lord in the air. And thus we shall always be with the Lord.

I THESSALONIANS 4:16–17

"Let not your heart be troubled; you believe in God, believe also in Me. In My Father's house are many mansions; if it were not so, I would have told you. I go to prepare a place for you. And if I go and prepare a place for you, I will come again and receive you to Myself; that where I am, there you may be also."

JOHN 14:1–3

"The Son of Man will come in the glory of His Father with His angels, and then He will reward each according to his works."

MATTHEW 16:27

"Watch therefore, for you do not know what hour your Lord is coming. But know this, that if the master of the house had known what hour the thief would come, he would have watched and not allowed his house to be broken into. Therefore you also be ready, for the Son of Man is coming at an hour you do not expect."

MATTHEW 24:42–44

Behold, He is coming with clouds, and every eye will see Him, even they who pierced Him. And all the tribes of the earth will mourn because of Him. Even so, Amen.

"I am the Alpha and the Omega, the Beginning and the End," says the Lord, "who is and who was and who is to come, the Almighty."

REVELATION 1:7–8

Lord, You came first as the suffering Servant. You will return as the victorious King of kings. May I honor You in all I do, in every aspect of my life, as I await that glorious day. Amen.

49

GOD'S GIFT OF OUR HEAVENLY REWARD

B eing filled with the Lord's presence as we journey through life seems blessing enough for naming Jesus our Savior. But God also has an eternal reward for those of us who call Jesus Lord and who live to honor and glorify Him. In the following scriptures, we will read about *a crown of righteousness*, *pleasures forevermore*, and *a place* that Jesus Himself is preparing for us. The Lord promises to reward His people for their kingdom service, all of which He has seen even if others haven't. God blesses us richly in this life, but spending eternity with Him is the ultimate reward.

I have fought the good fight, I have finished the race, I have kept the faith. Finally, there is laid up for me the crown of righteousness, which the Lord, the righteous Judge, will give to me on that Day, and not to me only but also to all who have loved His appearing.

2 TIMOTHY 4:7–8

"Take heed that you do not do your charitable deeds before men, to be seen by them. Otherwise you have no reward from your Father in heaven. . . . But when you do a charitable deed, do not let your left hand know what your right hand is doing, that your charitable deed may be in secret; and your Father who sees in secret will Himself reward you openly."

MATTHEW 6:1, 3–4

"I am coming quickly, and My reward is with Me, to give to every one according to his work."

REVELATION 22:12

In Your presence is fullness of joy;
At Your right hand are pleasures
forevermore.

PSALM 16:11

"I go to prepare a place for you. And if I go and prepare a place for you, I will come again and receive you to Myself; that where I am, there you may be also."

JOHN 14:2–3

Father and King, I thank You for the rewards You have awaiting Your faithful people. May I live to receive what may be the greatest reward of all: knowing that I have been a faithful servant for You. Amen.

50

GOD'S GIFT OF ETERNAL LIFE

Among the many blessings of naming Jesus your Savior and Lord is the promise of eternal life with Him. That choice is yours and yours alone. Only you can acknowledge your sin, admit your need for a Savior, receive Jesus as that Savior, and live with Him as your Lord. Living with Him as Lord will determine life choices, both personal and professional. Are you turning to Him for guidance during this season of transition? Maybe first you need to turn to Him for forgiveness of sin and His welcome into His family. Only you know where you stand with Jesus.

"My sheep hear My voice, and I know them, and they follow Me. And I give them eternal life, and they shall never perish; neither shall anyone snatch them out of My hand. My Father, who has given them to Me, is greater than all; and no one is able to snatch them out of My Father's hand. I and My Father are one."

JOHN 10:27–30

"The hour has come that the Son of Man should be glorified. Most assuredly, I say to you, unless a grain of wheat falls into the ground and dies, it remains alone; but if it dies, it produces much grain. He who loves his life will lose it, and he who hates his life in this world will keep it for eternal life. If anyone serves Me, let him follow Me; and where I am, there My servant will be also. If anyone serves Me, him My Father will honor."

JOHN 12:23–26

"All the nations will be gathered before Him, and He will separate them one from another, as a shepherd divides his sheep from the goats. And He will set the sheep on His right hand, but the goats on the left. Then the King will say to those on His right hand, 'Come, you blessed of My Father, inherit the kingdom prepared for you from the foundation of the world: for I was hungry and you gave Me food; I was thirsty and you gave Me drink; I was a stranger and you took Me in; I was naked and you clothed Me; I was sick and you visited Me; I was in prison and you came to Me.'

"Then the righteous will answer Him, saying, 'Lord, when did we see You hungry and feed You, or thirsty and give You drink? When did we see You a stranger and take You in, or naked and clothe You? Or when did we see You sick, or in prison, and come to You?' And the King will answer and say to them, 'Assuredly, I say to you, inasmuch as you did it to one of the least of these My brethren, you did it to Me.'"

MATTHEW 25:32–40

173

"Whoever eats My flesh and drinks My blood has eternal life, and I will raise him up at the last day. For My flesh is food indeed, and My blood is drink indeed. He who eats My flesh and drinks My blood abides in Me, and I in him. As the living Father sent Me, and I live because of the Father, so he who feeds on Me will live because of Me. This is the bread which came down from heaven—not as your fathers ate the manna, and are dead. He who eats this bread will live forever."

JOHN 6:54–58

Jesus spoke these words, lifted up His eyes to heaven, and said: "Father, the hour has come. Glorify Your Son, that Your Son also may glorify You, as You have given Him authority over all flesh, that He should give eternal life to as many as You have given Him. And this is eternal life, that they may know You, the only true God, and Jesus Christ whom You have sent."

JOHN 17:1–3

174

Father, thank You for inviting me to join Your family. Thank You for forgiving my sins. Thank You for being my Shepherd as I journey through life and toward my eternal home with You. Amen.

51

GOD'S GIFT OF REPENTANCE

We sin when we fall short of God's standards and follow our own desires, not His. God graciously helps us recognize our sin. But merely acknowledging that our thoughts, words, and actions don't meet our holy God's standards is not enough. Our subsequent actions need to reflect our genuine recognition of how we have failed. Are we continuing with our sinful words and ways, or are we repenting, turning away from those sinful words and ways and turning toward God and His grace and mercy? Repenting of our sin brings us His forgiveness and genuine joy in His presence.

"Those who are well have no need of a physician, but those who are sick. I did not come to call the righteous, but sinners, to repentance."

MARK 2:17

Repent therefore and be converted, that your sins may be blotted out, so that times of refreshing may come from the presence of the Lord.

ACTS 3:19

If we say that we have no sin, we deceive ourselves, and the truth is not in us. If we confess our sins, He is faithful and just to forgive us our sins and to cleanse us from all unrighteousness. If we say that we have not sinned, we make Him a liar, and His word is not in us.

1 JOHN 1:8–10

"If My people who are called by My name will humble themselves, and pray and seek My face, and turn from their wicked ways, then I will hear from heaven, and will forgive their sin."

2 CHRONICLES 7:14

He who covers his sins will not prosper,
But whoever confesses and forsakes
them will have mercy.

PROVERBS 28:13

*Thank You for Your Holy Spirit who helps
me recognize my sin, for Your love that
moves me to confess my sin and repent,
and for Your gracious forgiveness that
welcomes me into Your family. Amen.*

52

GOD'S GIFT OF CONTENTMENT

God wants us to know peace; we too often choose stress and striving. God wants us to find satisfaction in Him; we too often look around and find ourselves wanting more. God wants us to give thanks for all we have; we too often focus on what we don't have. No wonder contentment is elusive! We're looking all around instead of at God. Whatever path you walk in this new chapter, looking into God's eyes and seeing His love for you—you are the apple of His eye (Psalm 17:8)—is the key to contentment whatever the circumstances of life.

I have learned in whatever state I am, to be content.

Let your conduct be without covetousness; be content with such things as you have. For He Himself has said, "I will never leave you nor forsake you."

HEBREWS 13:5

"Take heed and beware of covetousness, for one's life does not consist in the abundance of the things he possesses."

LUKE 12:15

Those who seek the Lord shall not lack any good thing.

PSALM 34:10

The Lord is my shepherd;
I shall not want.

PSALM 23:1

180

Lord, keeping my eyes on You is key to a life of contentment. Please help me find in You the joy and fulfillment You offer and the peace and contentment only You can give. Amen.